Merry Chr

Dear Nancy

Love Gary

in memories of England

THE HISTORY OF
THE TALE OF PETER RABBIT

THE HISTORY OF

THE TALE OF PETER RABBIT

Taken mainly from Leslie Linder's
A History of the Writings of Beatrix Potter
together with the text and illustrations
from the first privately printed edition

WITH EIGHT PLATES IN COLOUR
AND TEXT ILLUSTRATIONS IN
BLACK AND WHITE

FREDERICK WARNE

Published by
FREDERICK WARNE & CO LTD : LONDON
FREDERICK WARNE & CO INC : NEW YORK
1976

The Publishers dedicate this book to

LESLIE LINDER
without whose enthusiasm much of
Beatrix Potter's history and works
would have remained undiscovered

This book published
simultaneously in Canada by
Saunders of Toronto Limited
850 York Mills Road, Don Mills, Ontario M3B 2M8

LIBRARY OF CONGRESS CATALOG
CARD NO. 76–14117

ISBN 0 7232 1988 5

Printed in Great Britain by
William Clowes & Sons, Limited
London, Beccles and Colchester
725.676

CONTENTS

LIST OF COLOUR PLATES

INTRODUCTION

Seventy-five years ago, on December 16th, 1901, Peter Rabbit first appeared in print, and nearly a year later in October the first Warne edition was published. As these important anniversaries could not be allowed to slip by unnoticed Frederick Warne decided to publish a commemorative volume with as its major feature the entire text and illustrations of Beatrix Potter's first privately printed edition of *The Tale of Peter Rabbit*.

It is always intriguing to discover the story behind the story—what inspired the author to write it in the first place, the problems that occurred before—and after—it reached the publisher's office and its subsequent world-wide success. This book presents the history of *The Tale of Peter Rabbit*, told mainly in Leslie Linder's words from his *History of the Writings of Beatrix Potter* but adapted a little to suit the plan of this book.

THE PICTURE LETTER

When Beatrix Potter was nearly seventeen, Annie Carter, who was just turned twenty, came to Bolton Gardens to be her companion and to teach her German. They became devoted to each other, and when a year or two later Miss Carter married and became Mrs. Moore and went to live at Bayswater, Beatrix Potter kept in close touch with her.

It was at Bayswater that her first child, a boy, was born and called Noel because he arrived on Christmas Eve. The other seven children were born at Number

Twenty, Baskerville Road, Wandsworth Common, to which Mrs. Moore moved shortly after Noel's birth, and where she lived for the rest of her life.

Over the years Beatrix Potter visited her frequently. It was a red-letter day for the Moore children when she came to tea, for she arrived in a smart carriage and pair with a coachman on the box. Sometimes the carriage waited outside the house until the visit was over. On these occasions she often wore a straw hat with velvet ribbons tied under her chin.

The Moore family say she was pretty and gay, with sparkling blue eyes. Her voice was quiet and soft, though slightly higher in pitch than average. When she told of some amusing incident she gave a little twist to her mouth which, combined with a smile, they found quite fascinating.

She brought cages of white mice to show them; she used to open the door of the cage and let the mice run around the drawing-room floor, which their mother did not seem to mind.

Beatrix Potter became very fond of the children, and when five-year-old Noel became ill, she sent him a letter all about Peter Rabbit and his adventures in Mr. McGregor's garden.

It was at Eastwood, Dunkeld, a dower house on the Atholl Estate beside the River Tay that this picture letter was written on September 4th 1893. In 1905 Beatrix Potter wrote, 'It is much more satisfactory to address a real live child; I often think that that was the secret of the success of Peter Rabbit, it was written to a child—not made to order.'

Eastwood Dunkeld
Sep 4 93

My dear Noel,
          I don't know what to
write to you, so I shall tell you a story
          about four little rabbits
                    whose names were

Flopsy, Mopsy Cottontail

and Peter

They lived with their mother in a
sand bank under the root of a
big fir tree.

'Now, my dears', said old Mrs Bunny
'you may go into the field or down
the lane, but don't go into Mr McGregor's
garden.'

Flopsy, Mopsy & Cottontail, who were good
little rabbits went down the lane to gather
blackberries. but Peter, who was very naughty

ran straight away to Mr McGregor's garden
and squeezed underneath the gate.

First he ate some lettuce,
and some broad beans,
then some radishes, and
then, feeling rather sick,
he went to look for
some parsley; but
round the end of a
cucumber frame
whom should he meet but Mr McGregor!

Mr McGregor was planting out young cabbages
but he jumped up & ran after Peter waving
a rake & calling out 'Stop thief'!

Peter was most dreadfully frightened &
rushed. all over the garden for he had
forgotten the way back to the gate.
He lost one of his shoes among the cabbages

and the other shoe amongst the potatoes.
After losing them he ran on four legs &
went faster, so that I think he would

have got away altogether, if he had not
unfortunately run into a gooseberry net
and got caught fast by the large buttons
on his jacket. It was a blue jacket with
brass buttons, quite new.

Mr McGregor came up with a basket which
he intended to pop on the top of Peter,
but Peter wriggled out just in time,
leaving his jacket behind,

and this time he found the gate,
slipped underneath and ran home
safely.

Mr McGregor hung up the little jacket & shoes for a scarecrow, to frighten the black birds.

Peter was ill during the evening, in consequence of over eating himself. His mother put him to bed and gave him a dose of camomile tea,

but Flopsy, Mopsy, and Cottontail
had bread and milk and blackberries
for supper.   I am coming
back to London next Thursday, so
I hope I shall see you soon, and
the new baby   I remain, dear Noel,
yours affectionately
                    Beatrix Potter

THE HISTORY OF THE BOOKS

A few years after the Peter Rabbit letter had been sent to Noel, it occurred to Beatrix Potter that she might make a little book of the story, and she wrote to ask if Noel had kept the letter, and if so could she borrow it? Noel *had* kept the letter and was glad to lend it to her.

First she made pen-and-ink copies of the drawings on some folded sheets of thin paper, but they showed through on the reverse side so she started all over again, this time using notepaper. From this copy Beatrix Potter rewrote the story in a stiff-covered exercise book and prepared forty-two pen-and-ink drawings to illustrate it, which were tucked into corner slots in the pages of the book. It was called 'The Tale of Peter Rabbit and Mr. McGregor's Garden, by H. B. Potter.' In addition to the black-and-white drawings there was a coloured frontispiece, showing Peter in bed, and his mother, Mrs. Rabbit, giving him a cup of camomile tea.

Canon Rawnsley, a founder member of The National Trust, who was a friend of the family, became interested in Beatrix Potter's idea to make this story letter into a book. He offered to help her find a publisher and to submit the manuscript on her behalf.

During 1900 the story was sent to at least six publishers, from whom, one by one, it was returned with or without thanks. On March 13th 1900, in a picture letter to Marjorie Moore, Beatrix Potter told her she did not think her Peter Rabbit story would be made into a book this time. 'The Publisher is a gentleman who prints books, and he wants a bigger book than he has got enough money to pay for! and Miss Potter has arguments with him . . . I think Miss Potter will go off to another publisher soon . . . she would rather make two or three little books costing 1/- each than one big book costing 6/-, because she thinks little rabbits cannot afford to spend six shillings on one book.' The text of this letter was accompanied by a drawing of two little rabbits looking in a book-shop window, with one shilling each, and mother closing her purse.

Five weeks later, in a postscript to another picture letter, this time sent to Freda Moore, Beatrix Potter told her, 'Miss Potter is sitting upon her book at present and considering! The publisher cannot tell what has become of it.'

By 1901, however, there seemed no immediate prospects of finding a publisher, so Beatrix Potter made up her mind to have the story printed privately, and got in touch with a London printer called Strangeways & Sons, of Tower Street, Cambridge Circus, W.C., who had been recommended to her by her friend Miss Woodward of the Natural History Museum.

Canon Rawnsley, on the other hand, was still trying to get the Peter Rabbit story published. In September 1901 he wrote again to Frederick Warne & Co., one of the publishers who had previously been approached and had courteously declined to accept the book, offering them as an alternative his own version of the story, written in verse, to be illustrated by Beatrix Potter's drawings.

On the title page of his manuscript were the words 'The Tale of Peter Rabbit, written and illustrated by Beatrix Potter, done into rhyme by Canon Rawnsley', and by way of decoration, there was a silhouette of Peter.

The same size was used, and the story began:

> There were four little bunnies
> —no bunnies were sweeter
> Mopsy and Cotton-tail,
> Flopsy and Peter.
>
> They lived in a sand-bank
> as here you may see,
> At the foot of a fir
> —a magnificent tree.

and after proceeding, verse upon verse for some forty-one pages, ended with the moral:

> They sat down to tea
> Too good mannered to cram
> and ate bread and milk
> and sweet blackberry jam.
>
> And thought as we all
> think by far the best way
> To do what we're told
> and our mothers obey.

Frederick Warne & Co. in their reply to Canon Rawnsley on September 18th preferred the simple straightforward text of Beatrix Potter, and told him, 'As regards the letter-press, we think there is a great deal to be said for the simple narration ... though there are many good ideas in your verses which might be introduced with advantage.'

They hesitated as to the advisability of accepting the book, saying, 'moreover we are persuaded that to make the book a success it is absolutely necessary that the pictures should be coloured throughout', adding, 'Miss Potter seems to think the colour would be uninteresting.' She had told them, 'I did not colour the whole book for two reasons—the great expense of good colour printing—and also the rather uninteresting colour of a good many of the subjects which are most of them rabbit brown and green'; and summing up they said, 'as it is too late to produce a book for this season, we think it best to decline your kind offer at any rate for this year.' So for the time being nothing further happened.

It is clear that Frederick Warne & Co. had given careful consideration to the acceptance of *Peter Rabbit*, for in order to provide a practical lay-out for printing, they had gone to the trouble of marking with an 'E' the drawings which they considered should be eliminated without interfering with the story. There were 42 drawings in Beatrix Potter's manuscript. 'In our opinion', they wrote, 'the book would be best cut down to 32 pictures only, and each of these should be reproduced in colour.'

In the meantime Beatrix Potter was making progress with her privately printed edition. The coloured frontispiece had been produced by the recently introduced three-colour process, and Hentschel of 182, Fleet Street had made the required set of colour blocks and sent her 500 impressions. This was about twice the number required for the first printing, but Beatrix Potter was probably considering the likelihood of a second printing.

For the black-and-white illustrations she had 42 zinc blocks made by the Art Reproduction Company of Fetter Lane, E.C., excluding the block for the cover picture which was dealt with later.

The size of the book was to be in accordance with her own ideas of what a child's book should be like—small enough for little hands to hold, and printed on stout paper. The size she first suggested was $5 \times 3\frac{3}{4}$ inches (127 mm × 95 mm), which was the size of the manuscript she had sent to Warnes. The page was eventually made 135 mm × 103 mm, and due to the printing arrangement, it was only possible to include 41 of the 42 pictures which had been prepared.

The story was very like Noel's letter, except that it was longer, and there were more illustrations. On alternate pages a few lines of simple text faced each picture. The book was bound in paper boards cut flush, and the cover was of a subdued shade of grey-green on which there was a drawing of four little rabbits. The pages were unnumbered.

On December 16th 1901 this first privately printed edition of 250 copies was ready. Besides giving these books to her relations and friends, Beatrix Potter was selling them for the modest sum of 1/2d.

The Tale of Peter Rabbit (she had omitted 'and Mr. McGregor's Garden'), proved a success from the very first, and within a week or two Beatrix Potter decided to have a second impression of 200 copies in a slightly better binding with a rounded back. There were two or three changes in the punctuation, and a few changes to the text; also, in this second printing, the date 'February 1902' appeared on the title page, which had hitherto been undated. The cover was olive-green.

Apart from the small changes in punctuation, the alterations to the text were

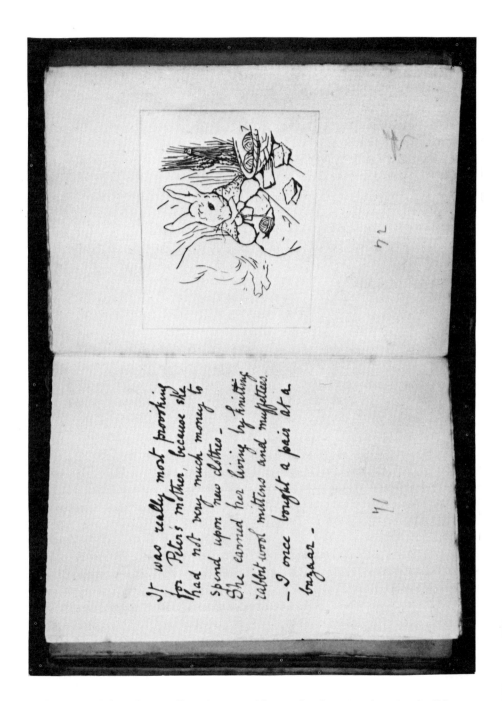

It was really most provoking for Peter's mother, because she had not very much money to spend upon new clothes —

She earned her living by knitting rabbit-wool mittens and mufflers. — I once bought a pair at a bazaar. —

Reproduced from Beatrix Potter's original layout for the privately printed edition as follows:

(Page numbers are counting from the first page of text)

Page	First Printing	Second Impression
51	She shook her head at him. Peter began to cry again.	She only shook her head at him. Peter began to cry again.
57	He went towards the tool-shed again, but suddenly there was a most peculiar noise—scr-r-ritch, scratch, scratch, scritch. Peter scuttered underneath the bushes. Then some one began to sing 'Three blind mice, three blind mice!' It sounded disagreeable to Peter; it made him feel as though his own tail were going to be cut off: his fur stood on end.	He went back towards the tool-shed, but suddenly, quite close to him, he heard the noise of a hoe—scr-r-ritch scratch, scratch, scratch. Peter scuttered underneath the bushes and hid. Then some one began to sing 'Three blind mice, three blind mice!' It sounded disagreeable to Peter: his fur stood on end.
59	After a time, as nothing happened, Peter came out, and climbed upon a wheel-barrow, and peeped over. The first thing he saw was Mr. McGregor hoeing onions. His back was turned towards Peter, and beyond him was the gate!	It made him feel as if his own tail were going to be cut off. But nothing happened; so presently Peter came out and climbed upon a wheel-barrow, and peeped over. The first thing he saw was Mr. McGregor hoeing onions. His back was turned towards Peter, and beyond him was the gate!

Before the first privately printed edition was ready Frederick Warne & Co. had reconsidered their previous decision, and, since Beatrix Potter was willing to prepare coloured illustrations throughout, they decided to accept *The Tale of Peter Rabbit*, subject to a satisfactory agreement being drawn up with regard to royalties. They wrote to her as follows:

To Miss Potter

December 16th 1901   London

Dear Miss Potter,

I must apologize for not having written to you earlier with reference to the 'Bunny Book'. I am now writing to Cumberland as I find I have mislaid your London address. I am sorry the estimate which I based on a first edition of 5,000 copies, did not turn out very well, as I find it only shows a possible royalty for author and artist of 1d per copy, which would amount to about £20 on this first edition. On subsequent editions, we should be able to pay 3d per copy royalty. If you would care for us to go on, on this basis we shall be very pleased to produce an edition of 5,000 copies at our own risk, in colours as we suggested. Of course we cannot tell whether the work is likely to run to a second edition or not, and therefore we fear it might not provide a reasonable remuneration for you. It is possible we might be able to issue the book at a slightly higher price, so as to yield a better royalty. We will look into this, if you wish it, but we think that the book would not be half so saleable at a higher price than 1/6d. Will you kindly let us hear what you think about the matter, so that we may come to a definite decision about it.

Yours faithfully,
Frederick Warne & Co.

To Frederick Warne & Co.

December 18th 1901   2, Bolton Gardens

Dear Sir,

I was on the point of posting the book, when I received your letter of December 16th.

I think Strangeways have printed it rather nicely. It is going off very well amongst my friends and relations, five at a time; I will spread it about as much as I can, especially in Manchester.

Had you decided *not* to go on with it, I would certainly have done so myself, it has given me so much amusement. I showed it this morning to some ladies who have a bookshop in Kensington, who wanted to put it in the window on the spot, but I did not venture to do so—though I would have been much interested.

I do not know if it is necessary to consult Canon Rawnsley; I should think *not*.

Speaking for myself, I consider your terms very liberal as regards royalty; but I do not quite understand about the copyright. Do you propose that the copyright remains mine; you agreeing to print an edition of 5,000, and having—as part of the agreement—the option of printing more editions if required? I must apologize for not understanding, but I would like to be clear about it. For instance who would the copyright belong to in the event of *your* not wishing to print a second edition? I am sure no one is likely to offer me better terms than 3d apiece, and I am aware that these little books don't last long, even if they are a success; but I should like to know what I am agreeing to.

I think it should certainly be kept down to 1/6, even if it took off my 1d. royalty on the first edition. I should be glad to call sometime at the office to hear what you decide about the coloured drawings. I still think the 3 colour photograph very nice, but I confess I had not thought of the plan of *brown* ink when I expressed such a strong dislike to black outlines—I have put a 'X' on some of the cuts which don't really seem to need alteration, but I am perfectly willing to re-draw the whole if desired.

I remain Sir,
yrs. sincerely,
Beatrix Potter

I have not spoken to Mr. Potter, but I think Sir, it would be well to explain the agreement clearly because he is a little formal having been a barrister.

It would appear that the colour process on which Warnes had based their first estimate was less costly than the three-colour process used by Hentschel for Beatrix Potter's Peter Rabbit frontispiece. Beatrix Potter wished them to use this three-colour process because she thought it would give the best results. Warnes therefore decided to prepare a further estimate and to reconsider their offer of December 16th.

In their letter of acknowledgement they wrote:

To Miss Potter

December 21st 1901   London

Dear Madam,

We have to acknowledge with thanks the receipt of your special edition of your quaint little book. It has been much admired by our representatives, who are just now home from their journeys, and we have no doubt that we should be able to do well with the coloured edition for next season.

With regard to the copyright, this would have to be ceded to us, but some clause could doubtless be inserted in the agreement by which in the event of our not deciding to issue a second edition, we would agree to transfer the copyright and blocks to you on payment of the original cost of the latter, or some agreed proportion thereof. You still seem rather to wish the plates to be engraved by the three colour process and we are therefore taking a new estimate. This will probably entail a considerable increase in the initial cost, but would we think give the most artistic result. We shall not have the particulars of this estimate for about a week, and we propose to write you again then fixing an appointment when perhaps you could kindly arrange to call and discuss with us the details of the agreement and form of the book.

With kind regards and wishing you all the compliments of the season

We are,

Yours faithfully,

Frederick Warne & Co.

P.S. We very much prefer your own letterpress to the verses by Canon Rawnsley.

By the end of the first week in January Beatrix Potter had not heard from Warnes about the new estimate, and we find her writing to them again, giving further information about Hentschel's three-colour blocks.

To Frederick Warne & Co.

January 7th 1902   2, Bolton Gardens

Dear Sir,

I send you another copy of Peter Rabbit—I did not remember to tell you when discussing Hentschel's blocks that the set I have got here in my possession seems to be particularly well finished.

I know a little about copper as my brother etches in it, and have some experience of printing—I work on stone myself but have never done coloured lithographs; but it is such an old-fashioned expensive method it would not have been of much use, even if I had been competent to work out my own drawings.

I think Hentschel would make the best job of it, if the money part of the business can be arranged, which I do not doubt it can be somehow.

I remain, Sir,

yrs. sincerely,

Beatrix Potter

The investigations into the additional cost of using the three-colour process took longer than at first expected, and it was not until May that Warnes submitted their revised proposals.

During the ensuing months, discussions took place on various matters relating to the book, as will be seen from the following correspondence.

To Frederick Warne & Co.

January 12th 1902   2, Bolton Gardens

Dear Sir,

I wrote to Hentschel to ask something about paint; and enquired at the same time about engraving very small blocks.

Two blocks can go inside their minimum of 20 sq. inch, and *if drawn on one sheet of paper* can be photographed together, with an extra 1/- each for dividing and mounting.

I work that out, 16 pairs at £3.3 + 2/- for mounting = £52.—Their charge is 3/6 per sq. inch. I do not clearly understand whether they would be willing to photograph a larger number than 2 together, which might effect a further saving.

I did not mention your name, having no authority to write to them—

In case you have written to them and got a similar proposal I thought I would tell you I am quite willing to copy the drawings in groups if required. There is no use beginning to colour them until I know.

I was wondering, if you are too busy to attend to it at present, whether you would care for me to call at Hentschel's—without of course any authority to make a bargain—to find out what they mean by the 3/6?

The drawings must have ½ inch clear space round each; if a number could be photographed at once, and *if the ½ inch between is* NOT *charged for*, it would seem rather reasonable—under £40(?)

The £52 is less than I guessed; but more than your other estimate; but I thought you said Evans charged 4/6.

I remain, Sir,
yrs sincerely,
Beatrix Potter

I calculated the blocks at their present size.

To Miss Potter

January 13th 1902 London

Dear Madam,

We have already made enquiries of Messrs Hentschel, and still wait further information from them, on receipt of which we will again write to you on the subject of preparing your designs for reproduction. We hope to have full particulars on Wednesday next, and we do not think it will be necessary for you to call at Hentschel's as suggested in your letter, as we shall be able to send you the necessary information to effect economy in making the blocks.

We are, Dear Madam,
Yours faithfully,
Frederick Warne & Co.

*NDW**

To Miss Potter

January 17th 1902 London

Dear Madam,

Peter Rabbit

In further reference to your letter of 12th inst, we have now ascertained particulars of Hentschel's respecting the best method of preparing your designs to economise in cost of reproduction.

A saving can be effected by making two or perhaps three drawings on one sheet of paper, but to what extent depends upon the actual sizes of the blocks, and as we have not a copy of the book before us it is somewhat difficult to determine whether two or three drawings should be grouped. Also if it is your intention to prepare your designs with a view to reduction it would be necessary to have them drawn to reduce to the same scale.

The grouping arrangement could be very easily dealt with if we had the entire set of pictures, and we would suggest that you prepare the drawings *singly* and allow us to cut down the margin of paper and neatly mount them in groups whereby so doing, a saving can be effected.

With regard to the cost of the blocks, we are quoted the price you state, *viz.* 3/6 per square inch, but for separating the price quoted is 1/6 per block. The margin between each drawing is included in the calculation of square inches and is charged for.

We trust you will now be able to proceed with the drawings, but should you desire further information, we shall be glad if you would call and see us.

We are,
Yours faithfully,
Frederick Warne & Co.

NDW

* Some letters from Frederick Warne & Co. were initialled *NDW* (Norman Dalziel Warne).

January 19th 1902   2, Bolton Gardens

Dear Sir,

I return the marked copy of Peter Rabbit—The present blocks are all within $2\frac{1}{2} \times 3$ (some are being reckoned sideways). I find that 15 were reduced by $\frac{1}{3}$ and 17 by $\frac{1}{4}$.

I don't think this would signify, provided that the right sizes were mounted together in the way you suggest.

I suppose that you will not be doing anything just at present, with those already coloured. I think there was some paint used in some of them which would be better taken out before they are photographed.

The shapes of the zinc blocks, and also of coloured drawings which you already have, were rather irregular.

Perhaps you will consider whether you prefer a variety of shape (within a certain size)— or whether you would like the backgrounds worked up to make a more uniform shape.

I shall be very glad to prepare the drawings in any way to suit your convenience: I will set to work to colour the others and will bring them to the office—

I cannot call this next week as I am going into the country, but I can get on with the work now that it is definitely decided which process is to be used.

I remain, Sir,
yrs. sincerely,
Beatrix Potter

I do not know if it is worth mentioning—But Dr. Conan Doyle had a copy for his children and he has a good opinion of the story and words.

Beatrix Potter was now planning the text and illustrations for her book. She was using one of the flat-backed privately printed editions as a working copy; on the cover she had pencilled 'Working Copy, 2 Bolton Gdns. S.W.'

First she looked carefully through the illustrations to decide which ones should be left out. Warnes had now restricted her to thirty, plus the frontispiece, so she had to take out eleven. These were crossed through in pencil, and the corresponding text transferred to other pages: in six cases to the following page; in two cases to the previous page; and in some cases, the text was deleted altogether.

The text which had been transferred was neatly written in ink on the appropriate pages, and the pictures which she decided to use were numbered 1 to 30. Beatrix Potter then hand-coloured three of the black-and-white illustrations—to see how they would look when coloured. On each picture she had lightly pencilled the reduction, $\frac{1}{4}$ or $\frac{1}{3}$, as a guide when preparing her new drawings in groups to facilitate block-making.

Apart from the deletions and one or two alterations the text for the Warne *Peter Rabbit* was practically the same as that of her second privately printed edition. The deletions and major alterations are listed here.

'Peter gave himself up for lost and cried big tears' was altered to 'and wept big tears'. (Later this was altered again to 'shed big tears' in the fourth printing.)

The following sentences were deleted: 'There surely never *was* such a garden for cabbages! Hundreds and hundreds of them; and Peter was not tall enough to see over them, and felt too sick to eat them. It was just like a very bad dream!'

'In the middle of the garden he came to a pond' was changed to: 'Presently, he came to a pond'. (This alteration was made at proof stage.)

The 'scr-r-ritch, scratch, scratch, scritch' noise of the hoe which appeared in the first privately printed edition was retained, and to 'Peter scuttered underneath the bushes' were added the words 'and hid'. The following passages were deleted: 'Then some one began to sing "Three blind mice, three blind mice!" It sounded disagreeable to Peter: his fur stood on end.

'It made him feel as though his own tail were going to be cut off.'

'But nothing happened, so presently Peter came out, was altered to: 'But presently, as nothing happened, he came out'.

The following sentences were deleted and some were transferred later to *The Tale of Benjamin Bunny*, published in 1904: 'It was really most provoking for Peter's Mother, because she had not very much money to spend upon new clothes. She earned her living by knitting rabbit-wool mittens and muffettees. I once bought a pair at a bazaar.

'She also had a little field in which she grew herbs and rabbit tobacco (which is what we call lavender). She hung it up to dry in the kitchen in bunches, which she sold for a penny apiece to her rabbit neighbours in the warren.

'Did you ever see a little old buck-rabbit enjoying a pipe of rabbit-tobacco?'

And finally the words 'in consequence of having eaten too much in Mr. McGregor's garden' were deleted from the sentence beginning: 'I am sorry to say Peter was not very well during the evening'.

By the end of April good progress had been made with the preparation of the book, and the correspondence which follows covers many aspects of this work.

To Frederick Warne & Co.

April 25th 1902   2, Bolton Gardens

Dear Sir,

I think this is the drawing that Mr. Warne was looking for yesterday; the gardener seemed to be better in the drawing I brought yesterday, but I hope you will use which ever you like.

I have been wondering whether the rabbit on the cover ought not to face the other way, towards the binding; it would not take long to copy again—

I should like to take the opportunity of saying that I shall not be surprised or disappointed to hear that the figures work out badly for the first edition of Peter Rabbit.

I remain Sir,
yrs. sincerely,
Beatrix Potter

To Frederick Warne & Co.

April 30th 1902   2, Bolton Gardens

Dear Sir,

I am very sorry that I cannot call as I am going to Scotland to-morrow morning, my brother has made his arrangements and I don't want to miss travelling with him.

It is most provoking that I could not see the drawings before going, as I think I could very likely do them better there, as there is a garden—

Would you be so kind as to post me the two that are the worst? I should be very glad to try them again; any that you are not satisfied with—

The address will be Kalemouth, Roxburgh. I expect to be at home again in a fortnight and shall hope to call then at the office to hear what can be settled—

The book seems to go on of itself. I had requests for 9 copies yesterday from 3 people I do not know.

I remain,
yrs. sincerely,
Beatrix Potter

To Frederick Warne & Co.

May 2nd 1902   Kalemouth, Roxburgh

Dear Sir,

I have received the drawings and will do my best to make the alterations, I think they are all very reasonable criticisms.

My brother is sarcastic about the figures; what you and he take for Mr. McGregor's nose, was intended for his ear, not his nose at all.

I have written for some 'Albumen' and will set to work at once—

The people are very suitable here, if one was not afraid of them; especially the cook. If I cannot manage any other way, I will photograph her in the right position and copy the photograph—I never learnt to draw figures, but it is much more satisfactory to have another try at them and I am very glad that you have sent them back.

Believe me,
yrs. sincerely,
Beatrix Potter.

The rabbits will be no difficulty. I had exactly the same opinion about the one under the gate, and those with the kettle.

To Miss Potter

May 7th 1902   London

Dear Miss Potter,

We have now gone carefully into the estimates of *Peter Rabbit* and find that it will be necessary for us to produce a first edition of 6,000 copies. We propose to issue the book at 1/- net, with art paper cover as already submitted to you,—and at 1/6d net, bound in cloth. Initial expenses, as we feared, are rather heavy under the new method of producing blocks, and we should therefore have to ask you to allow us to have the first 3,000 copies of the 1/- edition, free of royalty. As regards the remainder, we propose to offer you a royalty of 10% on the published price. This would bring you in about 1¼d per copy on all 1/- copies sold after the first 3,000 and about 1⅞d on all 1/6d copies sold.

If these terms will be satisfactory to you, you might let us know and we will have an agreement drawn up on these lines to submit to you when you return to London.

We shall be glad to have remaining illustrations for the book as soon as possible so that we may have samples in good time for our travellers.

With kind regards,
Yours faithfully,
Frederick Warne & Co.

NDW

To Frederick Warne & Co.

May 8th 1902   Kalemouth, Roxburgh

Dear Sir,

I enclose the drawings. I fear it is not of much use posting on Friday, but if any further alteration is required, you might have time to post them back here this week.

If there had been time, I should like to have copied a photograph for 'Mrs. McGregor'; I have taken a very suitable person but cannot develop it here.

I think if you would kindly—as you suggest—draw out a rough draft of the agreement, and allow me to call at Bedford Street in order to hear it explained, it would be the best plan.

The royalty upon the 1st edition of 6,000 which you offer in your letter of May 7th is quite as much as I expected.

I should wish, before signing an agreement, to understand clearly what arrangement it would imply about the copyright; and what stipulations would be made about subsequent editions if required.

I am very glad to hear that the book can be sold as cheap as 1/- net; I should think at that price a large number will sell.

I wish that the drawings had been better; I dare say they may look better when reduced; but I am becoming so tired of them, I begin to think they are positively bad. I am sorry they have made such a muddle of them.

'Peter' died at 9 years old, just before I began the drawings and now when they are finished I have got another rabbit, and the drawings look wrong.

I remain, Sir,
yrs. sincerely,
Beatrix Potter

In due course, the remaining drawings were sent to Warnes and the blocks made. On May 22nd Beatrix Potter wrote from Bolton Gardens saying, 'Perhaps you will kindly send a line when the proofs come, and I will call. I shall be very much interested to see them', adding in a postscript: 'If my father happens to insist on going with me to see the agreement, would you please not mind him very much, if he is very fidgety about things—I am afraid it is not a very respectful way of talking and I don't wish to refer to it again, but I think it is better to mention before-hand he is sometimes a little difficult; I can of course do what I like about the book being 36. I suppose it is a habit of old gentlemen, but sometimes rather trying.'

To Miss Potter

June 2nd 1902 London

Dear Miss Potter,

I am sending you herewith proofs of the first four blocks received for *Peter Rabbit* with the originals. I shall be obliged if you will return all to me, with your criticisms, at your earliest convenience. I hope the others will be coming shortly.

Yours faithfully,
Norman D. Warne

P.S. We shall want the originals back as well as the proofs to guide our printers.

To Frederick Warne & Co.

June 4th 1902 2, Bolton Gardens

Dear Sir,

I think that Mr. McGregor and the single figure have been done as well as they possibly could—The *blue* block seems rather heavy in the other pair, for some reason.

If you thought of asking them to do anything further to the blocks—I would suggest filing out the blackberry at the top right hand corner; and toning down the *blue* in the green, on the *left* side only, of the fir tree.

The ground between the middle rabbit and the blackbird might be lighter with advantage. They are such small points that if you are satisfied with the blocks I hope that you will not trouble about them, from my mentioning them.

I think they have done more work on the lighter pair; both upon the cucumber frame, and in filing the edges.

I like the fir-tree plate the least, but I think if that green could be taken down it would be much less confused.

Thanking you very much for sending them,

believe me,

yrs. sincerely,

Beatrix Potter

To Frederick Warne & Co.

June 8th 1902   2, Bolton Gardens

Dear Sir,

I put some white paint on the leaves behind the wheel barrow but it did not seem an improvement so I have taken it off again.

If I have put in too much on any of the others you would find that it is easy to wipe it off.

yrs. sincerely,

Beatrix Potter

By the end of June the Peter Rabbit colour blocks were finished and a set of proofs was sent to Beatrix Potter for her comments.

To Miss Potter

June 24th 1902   London

Dear Miss Potter,

I have at last received the remaining eight proofs of *Peter Rabbit* from Hentschels, and send you set herewith for your inspection. I do not think this lot are quite so satisfactory on the whole as the first, but I do not know that very much can be done to improve them. Perhaps you will make any suggestions you think fit as you did with the earlier proofs, when we will get them attended to.

We have also received from Hentschels the revised proofs of the earlier blocks. We have gone over these very carefully and find that they have carried out your wishes as regards alterations, very successfully on the whole. We are not therefore sending these again for your inspection.

We also send you in same parcel proofs in various coloured papers of the proposed cover design. We shall be glad if you would select say 2 colours from the specimens sent you. We have marked two on the back which we prefer ourselves, but are quite willing to leave the final decision to you if you like any of the others better. I send a placed copy showing how the letterpress would appear in the finished book. You will notice that I have not pasted in four of the plates, namely No. 29, 27, 23 and 20. This is because Hentschels have only sent me one proof of these, which I reserved for your corrections.

I shall be glad if you will kindly look over the letterpress and say whether it is exactly as you wish. Please let us hear from you as soon as possible, so that we may get the book complete in the printers' hands.

Yours faithfully,

Frederick Warne & Co.

NDW

To Frederick Warne & Co.

June 29th 1902   2, Bolton Gardens

Dear Sir,

The letter about the book cover came here after I had gone to Bedford Street. I did not understand I was to pick out 2 colours. I would choose the two that were marked, and if you at all prefer the brown, I think it looked very well. I liked the green a little better, but perhaps

there are fewer brown books—They both went equally well with the colour of the rabbit—
yrs sincerely,
Beatrix Potter.

The final choice fell on grey and brown. The first proofs of *The Tale of Peter Rabbit* were expected in a few weeks, and Beatrix Potter was looking forward to seeing one.

To Frederick Warne & Co.

July 15th 1902   2, Bolton Gardens

Dear Mr. Warne,
    If you send my rabbit book would you be so kind as to mark it to be forwarded, or else direct it to Ees Wyke, Sawrey, Lancashire? We go to the Lakes for 3 months tomorrow, and it would be a long time to wait. . . .

Beatrix Potter's letters were becoming more personal, and the rest of this letter is about a new idea—a book of Nursery Rhymes which she would try to do better than Peter Rabbit.
    The printer's order for the first edition of *The Tale of Peter Rabbit* was placed on July 23rd, and in due course a set of proofs was sent.

To Miss Potter

August 16th 1902   London

Dear Miss Potter,
    We send you herewith a first proof from press of the colour plates of *Peter Rabbit*, also a rough proof of the letterpress, showing you how it will fall. We shall be glad if you will kindly read this over, and see if it is all in order, before we finally go to press.
    Our printers advise us they have found it rather difficult to register the blocks on the large sheet, but on the whole we think you will find they have not come out badly. We are going carefully over the sheet, with a view to getting them to improve the stock as they go along.
    The plate slipped in, in front of the half title page, is the one we propose to use for pasting on the cover.
With kind regards,
Yours faithfully,
Frederick Warne & Co.

NDW

To Frederick Warne & Co.

August 17th 1902   Ees Wyke, Sawrey

Dear Sir,
    I return the proofs of Peter Rabbit, the only alterations I would like to suggest—there is a full stop on page 27, where there ought to be a comma.
    On page 75, it might read better if another line were crossed out, I have marked it in pencil; or if that is inconvenient you might print it 'straight across the *cabbages*'. The word 'garden' has come twice close together owing to some lines having been cut out.
    The blocks do not seem to have registered quite exactly but the only two that seem really unpleasant are pages 65 and 74.
    As long as it does not become worse, I rather like the effect in some of them; it makes them softer. I think your printer has succeeded much better with the greens than Hentschel

32

This illustration of Peter Rabbit appeared on the cover and page *26* of the first Warne edition. It was removed from the story after the fourth printing, but was retained for the cover

It is believed that this version of the cover illustration, reproduced here in its actual size, was never used for the book

Plate 1

Plate 2   The frontispiece for both the privately printed edition and the Warne
edition, reproduced here actual size from the original artwork

Plate 3   'Now, my dears,' said Old Mrs. Rabbit one morning, 'you may go into the fields or down the lane, but don't go into Mr. McGregor's garden.'

Reproduced actual size from the original artwork

This picture of Mrs. McGregor and the pie containing Peter Rabbit's father was never used in the book because the publishers did not like the old woman's face

This younger version of Mrs. McGregor, reproduced from the first Warne edition, is probably a caricature of Beatrix Potter herself. It was removed after the fourth printing

Plate 4

Plate 5 'Mr. McGregor was quite sure that Peter was somewhere in the tool-shed, perhaps hidden underneath a flower-pot.'

Reproduced actual size from the original artwork

'After a time he began to wander about, going lippity—lippity—not very fast, and looking all round.

'He found a door in a wall; but it was locked, and there was no room for a fat little rabbit to squeeze underneath.'

'Peter never stopped running or looked behind him till he got home to the big fir-tree.'

These two illustrations, reproduced from a copy of the first Warne edition, were dropped after the fourth printing

Plate 6

Plate 7 'But Flopsy, Mopsy, and Cotton-tail had bread and milk and blackberries for supper.'

Reproduced actual size from the original artwork

Plate 8   Peter Rabbit's later career

This illustration was used in early printings of *The Tale of the Flopsy Bunnies* but was replaced, probably in the third printing, by a picture without a noticeboard because of the problem of English lettering in foreign editions

did; I hope the little book will be a success, there seems to be a great deal of trouble being taken with it.

It is a disappointing summer for work out of doors, I cannot get on at all so far.

I remain,

yrs. sincerely,

Beatrix Potter

Beatrix Potter's copy in the ordinary 1/- binding is inscribed '1st Edition. Oct. 2nd. 02', and a copy of the 1/6d cloth binding, with Rupert Potter's book plate, bears the date 'Oct. 02'.

We are told that orders for the entire first printing (8,000) were received prior to publication. The printers were Edmund Evans, The Racquet Court Press, Swan Street, London, E.C.

It is interesting to note that, according to Warne's records, the cost of labour, material, and royalty for the ordinary 1/- binding, was $5\frac{3}{4}$d per book—sheet and royalty $3\frac{11}{16}$d, cover paper $\frac{3}{16}$d and binding $1\frac{7}{8}$d.

By the end of 1902 over 28,000 copies had been printed, and in two years the number had risen to over 86,000.

In a questionnaire sent to Beatrix Potter in 1939, she recalled some of the details of the early printings of *The Tale of Peter Rabbit*, and wrote, 'There were two colours, both subdued inoffensive colours, used for binding the first impression of Peter. I have two more early impressions, still with the leaf endpapers, and the portrait of Mrs. M. (or myself) holding a pie. One bound in a stronger brown is either 2nd. or 3rd. printing. Another with a stronger green (I remember we couldn't match the two soft colours which I liked), this green one still has Mrs. McGregor and the leaf pattern endpaper and the word "shed" [in place of 'wept'] on page 51—I had marked it 4th. It must have been printed during 1903; before the date in 1903 when the Tailor and Squirrel Nutkin came out.'

After the fourth printing, the picture of Mrs. McGregor and the pie was removed, together with three other pictures including the picture which was also used for the cover, to make room for the new coloured pictorial end-papers, which were first introduced in the autumn of 1903 when *The Tale of Squirrel Nutkin* and *The Tailor of Gloucester* were first published.

Beatrix Potter's reference to this picture as being one of 'Mrs. M. (or myself)', is of interest. The drawing of Mrs. McGregor in the privately printed edition is of a rugged old country woman, and a similar, but coloured drawing was submitted to Warnes for *The Tale of Peter Rabbit*. They did not like it, and at the foot of the drawing wrote, 'We still do not like the old woman's face. Will you please have another try at this'. So possibly the young woman who appears as Mrs. McGregor on page 14 of Warne's edition is, after all, a caricature of Beatrix Potter herself, though not a very flattering one!

By 1907 the colour blocks of *The Tale of Peter Rabbit* had become worn, and in the autumn of that year they were renewed. In Beatrix Potter's copy of this printing, she wrote, 'New plates, Autumn 1907. Early copy, to be kept. H.B.P.'

Also, on an inserted slip of paper are the words 'New blocks, first time of re-engraving. First printing—see p. 68.' On page 68 there is a different picture of Peter in the wheel-barrow and Mr. McGregor in the distance hoeing onions—both Peter and Mr. McGregor are drawn much larger. Also, the picture of Mrs. Rabbit pouring out Peter's camomile tea on page 81, is more pleasing than the earlier one. These two blocks were in use for six or seven years, after which replacement blocks were made from the first edition pictures.

It was unfortunate that Warnes did not copyright *The Tale of Peter Rabbit* in America when it first came out. The result was that in 1904, a pirated edition appeared, published by Henry Altemus & Co. It was the same format as the Warne edition, and the pictures and text were copied from the fourth printing of 1903. There was nothing Warnes could do about it, and later, more pirated editions of Peter Rabbit appeared. One of these contained puzzle pictures with hidden animals for the children to discover, while another was made up into a set of Peter Rabbit cut-outs.

As early as 1907 Warnes were considering the possibility of translating some of Beatrix Potter's books into French and German. Apparently a French translation was made by an English person, but Beatrix Potter did not think very highly of it, for in September 1907 she wrote to Warnes saying, 'That French is choke full of mistakes both in spelling and grammar. I dare say it is the English type-writer's slip-shod reading of the M.S.S.; but we shall have to have the proof sheets read very carefully. I don't think it is nearly such a good rendering as the German; it is too English and rather *flat* for French. I should think a French person would tell the story in the present tense with many exclamation marks. I will ask my cousin to read it over.'

Nothing more appears to have developed in regard to foreign translations until the 1912 season, when the first two of Beatrix Potter's foreign translations were actually published. They were in Dutch, and were *The Tale of Peter Rabbit* and *The Tale of Jemima Puddle-Duck*—published under licence by Nijgh & Van Ditmar's Uitgevers-Maatschappij of Rotterdam, in November, 1912.

Also about that time at least three different French translators were approached by Frederick Warne & Co., one of which was Mlle Victorine Ballon, a teacher in a French school.

In a letter dated May 15th 1912 Beatrix Potter told Harold Warne, 'Mlle Ballon's translations are infinitely better than the others ... I still don't like the Peter completely ... I have written direct to Mlle B. to thank her for the amusement she has given me—and I have told her I like another "Peter" better; by *"une Anglaise"*, and requiring French correction—if she guesses it is my own, very likely she might offer to look it over—Something between mine and hers would be excellent. I said of course I had nothing to do with business arrangements; but I would tell you *I* am pleased with her French. It is just right—colloquial without being slangy ... I am keeping the French for the present—there may be a question of altering one or two names.' In a postscript, she added, 'You had better find out if her charge is reasonable, and then she and I could settle the text between us.'

The various translations, including the one by *une Anglaise* were worked on by Mlle Ballon and Jullienne Profichet, another teacher who had assisted her, and in due course they were returned to Beatrix Potter for her approval.

On November 11th 1912 Beatrix Potter wrote to Harold Warne and told him, 'The improved translation of Peter is very good and spirited. I think Mrs. Tiggy is perfectly charming in French. I hope you may decide to print *Peter, Jemima* and *Tiggy*...'

This work was now put in hand, and at the beginning of 1913 Beatrix Potter was sent some of the printer's proofs. 'I have gone through the French proofs,' she wrote on March 3rd, 'and will send one copy to the schoolmistress and suggest she might correct it in the Easter holidays—The *printers* have made very few mistakes.'

Later in April Mlle Ballon sent back the proofs, and various discussions took place; in particular about the names of the characters. 'Could the translator suggest French names instead of Flopsy, Mopsy and Mr. McGregor?' wrote Beatrix Potter. 'Madame Lapin and Queue-de-Coton sound all right.' So the names of the four little rabbits became, 'Flopsaut, Trotsaut, Queue-de-Coton et Pierre'; but Mr. 'Mac Grégor' hardly changed at all.

The corrected proofs were duly returned to Mr. Warne, and Beatrix Potter then discussed future procedure: 'The question of how many books to start with is rather for *you*', she wrote. 'Personally I should like to see the five launched at the same time—because myself I thought 'Sophie Canétang' and 'Poupette-à-l'Epingle' are more pleasing than the rabbits; and I should think it might be an advantage for your traveller to be able to offer an assortment of these little books *as they are said to be something new* in France. There may not be a stock of similar sized books for them to be added to as in England.' (The five titles to which Beatrix Potter was referring were *Peter Rabbit, Benjamin Bunny, Mrs. Tiggy-Winkle, Jemima Puddle-Duck* and *The Flopsy Bunnies*.)

The question of suitable end-papers and of amendments to certain pictures in which writing occurred had also to be discussed '... and no reading on any end-paper or pictures', wrote Beatrix Potter.

In the case of the end-papers, however, apart from using plain end-papers for some of the early printings, the existing ones with English titles on the little volumes were used. Beatrix Potter did, however, prepare a pair of end-paper designs without any lettering on them, but they were apparently never used.

In May 1913 an advance copy of *The Tale of Peter Rabbit* in French was ready. 'The French Peter looks well,' said Beatrix Potter, 'and is very amusing.' But for some time after this nothing more was done, and it wasn't until 1921 that *Pierre Lapin* was published.

Since then *Peter Rabbit* has become very cosmopolitan, appearing in Afrikaans (1929), Spanish (1931), Welsh (1932), German (1934 and 1972), Swedish (1948 and 1972), Italian (1948), Dutch again (1968), Japanese (1971), Norwegian (1972), Danish (1972) and even Latin (1962). Peter can also be read in i.t.a. and braille.

'I have never quite understood the secret of Peter's perennial charm,' wrote Beatrix Potter in 1940. 'Perhaps it is because he and his little friends keep on their

'The Rabbits' Potting Shed'   Bedwell Lodge, Hertfordshire, 1891
This potting-shed at Bedwell Lodge was also the tool-shed in *The Tale of Peter Rabbit*
(see Plate 5)

36

way; busily absorbed in their own doings. They were always independent. Like Topsy—they just "grow'd"—Their names especially seemed to be inevitable. I never knew a gardener named "Mr. McGregor". Several bearded horticulturalists have resented the nickname; but I do not know how it came about, nor why "Peter" was called Peter. It is regrettable that a small boy in church once inquired audibly whether the Apostle was Peter Rabbit? There is difficulty in finding or inventing names entirely new, void of all possible embarrassment.'

From her writings in her Journal and from her correspondence to Norman Warne we learn that her own pet rabbit was called Peter.

In one of her privately printed copies of *The Tale of Peter Rabbit*, Beatrix Potter wrote, 'In affectionate remembrance of poor old Peter Rabbit, who died on the 26th. of January 1901 at the end of his 9th. year. He was bought, at a very tender age, in the Uxbridge Road, Shepherds Bush, for the exorbitant sum of 4/6 ... whatever the limitations of his intellect or outward shortcomings of his fur, and his ears and toes, his disposition was uniformly amiable and his temper unfailingly sweet. An affectionate companion and a quiet friend.'

Other recollections of *The Tale of Peter Rabbit* are contained in a letter to Mr. Arthur Stephens of Frederick Warne, written in February 1942, in which Beatrix Potter tells how 'Peter was so composite and scattered in locality that I have found it troublesome to explain its various sources. If the vegetable garden and wicket gate were anywhere it was at Lingholm near Keswick; but it would be vain to look for it there, as a firm of landscape gardeners did away with it, and laid it out anew with paved walks etc. ... The lily pond in Peter was at Tenby, South Wales. The fir tree and some wood backgrounds were near Keswick. Mr.McGregor was no special person; unless in the rheumatic method of planting cabbages. I remember seeing a gardener in Berwickshire extended full length on his stomach weeding a carriage drive with a knife—his name I forget—not McGregor! I think the story was made up in Scotland ... Peter Rabbit's potting shed and actual geraniums were in Hertfordshire [at Bedwell Lodge, near Hatfield].'

The gardener in Berwickshire with whom she had associated Mr. McGregor, was in fact the gardener at Lennel near Coldstream, where the Potters spent the summer of 1894—but as this was a year *after* the Peter Rabbit story letter was written, it could not have been the origin of Mr. McGregor. It was at Lennel, on October 10th 1894, that Beatrix Potter wrote in her Journal, 'We were somewhat nettled during the last week by the activity of that idle person Mr. Hopkirk, the gardener, who made a frantic effort to get the place straight for his own employer after our departure. I have seen him lie flat on his face in a gravel walk, to weed with a little knife.'

In actual fact the Peter Rabbit picture letter was written in Mr. MacGregor's garden! for this was the name of the tenant who sub-let Eastwood to the Potters in 1893.

THE PRIVATELY PRINTED EDITION

Few people have had the opportunity of seeing Beatrix Potter's privately printed edition and comparing it with the Warne edition of *The Tale of Peter Rabbit* so it seemed appropriate to celebrate the 75th anniversary of its first appearance on December 16th, Peter's 'unofficial' birthday, by reissuing it in this history.

For reasons of space the pictures and relating text are on the same page, and the text has been reset.

THE TALE OF PETER RABBIT

ONCE upon a time there were four little Rabbits, and their names were—
Flopsy,
Mopsy,
Cotton-tail,
and Peter.

THEY lived with their Mother in a sand-bank, underneath the root of a very big fir-tree.

'NOW, my dears,' said old Mrs. Rabbit one morning, 'you may go into the fields or down the lane, but don't go into Mr. McGregor's garden.

'YOUR Father had an accident there; he was put in a pie by Mrs. McGregor.

'NOW run along, and don't get into mischief. I am going out.'

THEN old Mrs. Rabbit took a basket and her umbrella, and went through the wood to the baker's. She bought a loaf of brown bread and five currant buns.

FLOPSY, Mopsy, and Cotton-tail, who were good little bunnies, went down the lane to gather blackberries;

BUT Peter, who was very naughty, ran straight away to Mr. McGregor's garden,

AND squeezed under the gate!

FIRST he ate some lettuces and some broad beans;

AND then he ate some radishes;

AND then, feeling rather sick, he went to look for some parsley.

BUT round the end of a cucumber frame, whom should he meet but Mr. Mc-Gregor!

MR. McGREGOR was on his hands and knees planting out young cabbages, but he jumped up and ran after Peter, waving a rake and calling out, 'Stop thief!'

PETER was most dreadfully frightened; he rushed all over the garden, for he had forgotten the way back to the gate.

He lost one of his shoes among the cabbages,

AND the other shoe amongst the potatoes.

AFTER losing them, he ran on four legs and went faster, so that I think he might have got away altogether

IF he had not unfortunately run into a gooseberry net, and got caught by the large buttons on his jacket. It was a blue jacket with brass buttons, quite new.

PETER gave himself up for lost, and cried big tears; but his sobs were overheard by some friendly sparrows, who flew to him in great excitement, and implored him to exert himself.

MR. McGREGOR came up with a sieve, which he intended to pop upon the top of Peter; but Peter wriggled out just in time, leaving his jacket behind him,

AND rushed into the tool-shed, and jumped into a can. It would have been a beautiful thing to hide in, if it had not had so much water in it.

MR. McGREGOR was quite sure that Peter was somewhere in the tool-shed, perhaps hidden underneath a flower-pot. He began to turn them over carefully, looking under each.

Presently Peter sneezed—'Kertyschoo!' Mr. McGregor was after him in no time,

AND tried to put his foot upon Peter, who jumped out of a window, upsetting three plants. The window was too small for Mr. McGregor, and he was tired of running after Peter. He went back to his work.

PETER sat down to rest; he was out of breath and trembling with fright, and he had not the least idea which way to go. Also he was very damp with sitting in that can.

AFTER a time he began to wander about, going lippity—lippity—not very fast, and looking all round.

He found a door in a wall; but it was locked, and there was no room for a fat little rabbit to squeeze underneath.

AN old mouse was running in and out over the stone door-step, carrying peas and beans to her family in the wood. Peter asked her the way to the gate, but she had such a large pea in her mouth that she could not answer. She shook her head at him. Peter began to cry again.

THEN he tried to find his way straight across the garden, but he became more and more puzzled. There surely never *was* such a garden for cabbages! Hundreds and hundreds of them; and Peter was not tall enough to see over them, and felt too sick to eat them. It was just like a very bad dream!

IN the middle of the garden he came to a pond where Mr. McGregor filled his water-cans. A white cat was staring at some goldfish; she sat very, very still, but now and then the tip of her tail twitched as if it were alive. Peter thought it best to go away without speaking to her; he had heard about cats from his cousin, little Benjamin Bunny.

HE went towards the tool-shed again, but suddenly there was a most peculiar noise—scr-r-ritch, scratch, scratch, scritch. Peter scuttered underneath the bushes. Then some one began to sing 'Three blind mice, three blind mice!' It sounded disagreeable to Peter; it made him feel as though his own tail were going to be cut off: his fur stood on end.

AFTER a time, as nothing happened, Peter came out, and climbed upon a wheel-barrow, and peeped over. The first thing he saw was Mr. McGregor hoeing onions. His back was turned towards Peter, and beyond him was the gate!

PETER got down very quietly off the wheel-barrow, and started running as fast as he could go along a straight walk behind some blackcurrant bushes.

MR. McGREGOR caught sight of him at the corner, but Peter did not care. He slipped underneath the gate, and was safe at last in the wood outside the garden.

MR. McGREGOR hung up the little jacket and the shoes for a scare-crow to frighten the blackbirds.

PETER never stopped running or looked behind him till he got home to the big fir-tree.

HE was so tired that he flopped down upon the nice soft sand on the floor of the rabbit-hole, and shut his eyes. His Mother was busy cooking; she wondered what he had done with his clothes. It was the second little jacket and pair of shoes that Peter had lost in a fortnight!

IT was really most provoking for Peter's Mother, because she had not very much money to spend upon new clothes. She earned her living by knitting rabbit-wool mittens and muffettees. I once bought a pair at a bazaar.

SHE also had a little field in which she grew herbs and rabbit tobacco (this is what we call lavender). She hung it up to dry in the kitchen, in bunches, which she sold for a penny apiece to her rabbit neighbours in the warren.

DID you ever happen to see a little old buck-rabbit enjoying a pipe of rabbit-tobacco?

I AM sorry to say that Peter was not very well during the evening, in consequence of having eaten too much in Mr. McGregor's garden.

His Mother put him to bed, and made some camomile tea;

AND she gave a dose of it to Peter!
  'One table-spoonful to be taken at bed-time.'

BUT Flopsy, Mopsy, and Cotton-tail had bread and milk and blackberries for supper.

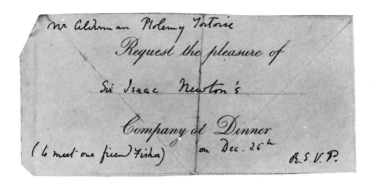

Mr Alderman Ptolemy Tortoise
Request the pleasure of
Sir Isaac Newton's
Company at Dinner
(to meet our friend Fisher) on Dec. 25th
R.S.V.P.

My dear Duchess,
If you are at home and not engaged will you come to tea tomorrow? but if you are away I shall put this in the post and invite cousin Tabitha Twitchit. There will be a red herring, & muffins & crumpets. The patty pans are all locked up. Do come.
yr aff friend Ribby—

Miss Duchess
Belle Green

Beatrix Potter wrote miniature letters as though they were from some of the animal characters in the books, and sent them to children she knew. They throw delightful sidelights on the characters and tell us more about them. They are collected together in *A History of the Tale of Beatrix Potter*

POSTSCRIPT

Demand for *The Tale of Peter Rabbit* never wanes. Judging by its popularity with its readers, it must be regarded as one of the best children's books ever created. But of course Peter's adventure doesn't end when he is put to bed and dosed with camomile tea, while his sisters Flopsy, Mopsy and Cotton-tail have bread and milk and blackberries for supper; Peter has a life-story, and it is most satisfying to be able to trace his history, and that of his sisters too, from book to book and through the miniature letters which Beatrix Potter encouraged her characters to write to each other—with a little bit of speculation here and there to add to the interest. . .

Peter's feud with Mr. McGregor was continued in *The Tale of Benjamin Bunny*, when the two young rabbits went to regain Peter's blue coat and shoes. The mission was accomplished, with their managing to acquire a handkerchief of onions, a tam o' shanter for Benjamin and a good beating apiece from Benjamin's father, Old Mr. Benjamin Bunny. The blue coat and red handkerchief turned up again amongst the washing in *The Tale of Mrs. Tiggy-Winkle*.

Nothing daunted, however, Peter was planning another daring campaign, with such audacity that it almost takes one's breath away. He actually wrote to Mr. McGregor to ask if his spring cabbages were ready (Miniature Letters in *A History of the Writings of Beatrix Potter*), and when he received a very 'ill written' reply from Mrs. McGregor to the effect that her husband who was 'in Bedd with a Cauld' would inform the 'Polisse', ending with a sinister threat about a new 'py-Dish' which was 'vary Large', Peter immediately contacted his cousin to arrange another raid.

We do not hear how this escapade ended, but they must have avoided the pie-dish fate because Peter and Benjamin are to be seen waiting patiently to be served in *Ginger and Pickles*. In fact Peter was a frequent customer. And our attention is drawn to the fact that Peter appears on the last page of *Pigling Bland* by some more of his correspondence, this time to a fortunate Master Drew Fayle.

But as is the case with many a wayward youth, Peter grew up to become quite a dependable rabbit and a good son to his mother, helping her run a business which was advertised in early editions of *The Flopsy Bunnies* as 'Peter Rabbit and Mother —Florists—Gardens neatly razed. Borders devastated by the night or year'. If Peter had a cabbage to spare he would often give his sister Flopsy a helping hand to feed her large family. There is interesting evidence in *The Art of Beatrix Potter* that a certain Benjamin Bunny was also in the vegetable business at one time, on the retail side, but as this was two years before Peter first ventured into Mr. McGregor's garden we assume that the greengrocer was Old Mr. Benjamin Bunny and that young Benjamin was the '& Son' of the partnership. He must have been a great disappointment to his father, though, because to avoid work he would hide himself in a barrel—to the big surprise of curious customers.*

We have a feeling that Peter remained a bachelor, for there is no mention of his taking a wife. In *Kitty-in-Boots*, which was never published as an individual book but appears in *A History of the Writings of Beatrix Potter*, there is a reference to a 'stout buck rabbit in a blue coat' who got the better of two objectionable ferrets by prodding them with his umbrella, and who used evasive tactics to escape being shot by Kitty. This surely must be Peter, more mature but as impudent as ever!

Peter's sister Flopsy married her cousin Benjamin, and they settled down to raise several children, all of whom seemed to be natural victims of the kidnapper: first there were the Flopsy Bunnies who, rightly enough, merited their own Tale when they were saved from becoming the lining to Mrs. McGregor's cloak largely through the efforts of Mrs. Thomasina Tittlemouse; and then another very young family who, though scarcely old enough to open their eyes, were carried off by Tommy Brock, through the carelessness of their paternal grandfather (renamed Old Mr. Bouncer) to an oven in the house belonging to Mr. Tod (whose Tale it also is). Luckily the oven was a cold one and they were rescued, thanks to Uncle Peter's level-headed advice to their panic-stricken father.

We learn from their Christmas Greetings to Master John Hough in *The Writings of Beatrix Potter*, that there were six Flopsy Bunnies, of varying ages and at varying stages of literacy. With such a large family Flopsy had to send washing out, and it is interesting to see that she chose the same washer-woman as her mother, Mrs. Josephine Rabbit, even though both ladies had cause for complaint against Mrs. Tiggy-Winkle, concerning her disorganised laundry methods (Miniature Letters again).

Cotton-tail was courted and won by a little black rabbit of a romantic but

---

* A cardboard picture which Beatrix Potter made in 1891 to amuse the children she knew. In this green-grocer's shop the lids of the basket and barrel could be raised, revealing apples in one, and a rabbit in the other.

retiring nature—he was wont to leave bunches of carrots outside Cotton-tail's door and then disappear (*Appley-Dapply's Nursery Rhymes*). They went to live on the hill and had a family of 'four or five' little rabbits, one favouring its father and the others brown like their mother. Cotton-tail and her husband did not believe in quarrelling with their neighbours and in *The Tale of Mr. Tod* were no help at all in rescuing Benjamin's babies.

And what of Mopsy? Sad to relate, we know nothing of Mopsy's life-story. We leave her cuddled comfortably, together with her sister Flopsy, in her mother's arms as quite a young rabbit at the end of *The Tale of Benjamin Bunny*. There are two little girl rabbits in pink capes in *Ginger and Pickles*, but no means of identifying Mopsy; they could just as easily be her sisters. Perhaps some accident befell her. . . Surely not another pie? No, she was much too good a rabbit to go anywhere near Mr. McGregor's garden.

Whatever happened to Mopsy?

A.E.